Us and Them?
Call in Frank, Dick and Jane!

How to Reenergize Your Company
with Honest, Clear Communication

Published by Granite-Collen Communications
P.O. Box 621, Camarillo, CA 93011

Library of Congress Data:

DiZazzo, Raymond
Us and Them? Call in Frank, Dick and Jane! How to Reenergize Your Company with Honest, Clear Communication

Raymond DiZazzo

ISBN: 0964880091
ISBN 13: 9780964880092

1. Business Communication.
2. Communication in Management
3. Personal Communication

Printed in the United States of America

Us and Them?
Call in Frank, Dick and Jane!
How to Reenergize Your Company with Honest, Clear Communication

Ray DiZazzo

Granite-Collen

Books by Ray DiZazzo

Convex and Concave:
The Mystery of the Magical Lenses

Washington's Salt

The Water Bulls

Moonmare

The Simian Bridge

Corporate Media Production

The Clarity Factor

Saying the Right Thing

Corporate Scriptwriting:
A Professional's Guide

Corporate Television:
A Producer's Handbook

The Car Buyer's Art:
How to Beat the Salesman at His Own Game
(with Darrel Parrish)

For Shawn Grennan, an amazing business executive,
a great communicator and a darn good guy.
And for Richard Dennis, a friend long gone
who inadvertently taught me,
among other important lessons,

the amazing power of communication.

Table of Contents

Forward

By Neal Spruce

President and CEO - Apex Fitness Group

When Ray DiZazzo came to Apex Fitness Group, I initially thought of him as a writer and training developer. It wasn't long, however, before we all realized that Ray could offer much more than words on paper and the ability to develop training. He was also a manager and a communicator with a special ability for making things clear and simple — qualities too often missing in standard corporate communication.

My Director of Operations also recognized Ray's unique qualities and put him to work in helping The Apex Fitness Group develop a corporate identity.

The timing was perfect.

Our company was rapidly expanding, making the need for 'tight' corporate communication, including vision and mission clarity, extremely important. 24 Hour Fitness, a major player in the fitness industry, was taking a serious interest in us, and a more and more complex and competitive marketplace was evolving around us. We knew we had to quickly expand the corporate structure, make sure our employees understood why we had done it, and set out on a course that everyone could understand and support.

Ray's development work was fast and effective. In much less time than I had expected we had developed a corporate I.D., clearly defining who we were and what we wanted to accomplish – in other words, a step-by-step path to success.

Ray and Alan Curtis, a second key executive of mine, polished our "Apex Fitness Corporate I.D." into a crystal clear, attractive "company bible" – a copy of which all employees received. In addition, Ray launched a series of communications to our local and remote employees (many lived in different parts of the country) to make sure that everyone was on the same page and crystal clear about my vision for the company.

As we then began to restructure Apex Fitness Group based on our new Corporate Identity, I was reminded that our Corporate Communications Department had been in need of an overhaul for some time. I asked Ray if he would like the challenge of "re-inventing" it, and he jumped at the chance.

For the next three years, during which time we became a part of the 24 Hour Fitness organization, Ray never ceased to amaze me with the quality and volume of work his group turned out. In a matter of a few months he had shaped the department into one of the most powerful and productive units in our company. When Ray left Apex to further pursue his writing, media and teaching passions, he left an indelible mark on all of us.

Ray's hard work remains intact in the fabric of our business. Our company messaging still lives within the communication framework that he established. And for that I will be eternally grateful.

–Neal Spruce

Introduction

As business leaders charged with the health and wellbeing of large and small companies, we are victims of an age-old, very damaging ailment. I call it the Us and Them Syndrome, and although we think of it as an attitude problem, in many ways it's like a disease. It quietly infects all levels of our management and hourly workforces causing continual "headaches", not to mention an assortment of other "feverish", "sluggish" and generally "painful" symptoms in many American companies.

Stop and think about it. Management and hourly will never see eye-to-eye, right? Many hourly people think managers spend their time with their feet up on a desk, pulling underhanded shenanigans in the ivory tower, and, if you happen to reside in the ivory tower, you probably believe those hourly people just can't be told the real truth. They don't understand business and they have no sense of the broad perspective that senior managers use to guide the organization. Sound about right? Us…and them.

Because of this syndrome we continually expend an enormous amount of time and energy working through a variety of productivity and general employee resistance problems. We also deal with a constant flow of destructive grapevine and rumor mill gossip. And let's not forget the underlying mistrust that we all harbor for the other side, along with the unspoken resentment. These are a few of the direct effects of the Us and Them Syndrome. The indirect effects may be difficult to measure, but we all know they are significant in terms of productivity losses and the ability to truly achieve a company's vision.

As destructive as the Us and Them Syndrome can be, it has two very interesting characteristics. First, to varying degrees it's a given in virtually all companies, so most businesses are at the same disadvantage – for the moment. Second, that disadvantage happens to be the case because managers *assume* the Us and Them Syndrome is the nature of the beast.

Well, here's some food for thought. *Bull!*

The Us and Them Syndrome is *not* a given, nor is it the nature of the beast. It can be "treated" and the companies who make it their business to do so and "get well" will find themselves at a tremendous advantage on the playing field. While their competitors trudge along in the mistaken belief that Us and Them just comes with the territory, these newly energized and focused companies will experience a greatly improved commitment to company goals, increased understanding on everyone's part of what it takes to be successful in business, and a new resurgence of the hard work and sense of urgency needed to propel a business to amazing heights.

Eliminating the Us and Them Syndrome is what this book is all about, and the medicine it prescribes is a return to the basics of honest, clear communication – a very simple, no punches pulled approach to clear communication that anyone in your business organization can understand and put to use. In fact, there's probably very little on these pages that you and your management team don't already know. The problem is, we don't know how to *use* what we know. Nor do we consider it a problem that requires our focus as a top priority. We've gotten so wrapped up in revenue models, productivity figures and profit projections, we've drifted away from the basic principles of simple, open communication, and one of many negative results is the Us and Them Syndrome.

Well, welcome back to Communication 101.

Part One of this book explores and carefully defines exactly what I mean when I refer to Frank, Dick and Jane as a metaphor for honest, clear communication. Part Two lays out a series of steps for putting the "Power Trio" (as I refer to Frank, Dick and Jane) to work in your organization. In Part Three you will find additional communication tips that will help you keep the Us and Them Syndrome from ever placing your company "under the weather" again.

Okay. Ready for some straight, simple, effective communication solutions?

Read on...

Part One:

Introducing Frank, Dick and Jane

One:

Been There, Done That - A Case Study

Think back. How many times have we each been a part of company programs, policies and general cultures that nurtured the Us and Them Syndrome? During my thirty year stint in the corporate world, I watched it happen so many times it often seemed like standard operating procedure! To consider one reason why, let's start with a classic Us and Them case study. The following account is based on a true story that took place in a very large telecommunications company I'll refer to as NuCom.

"Pay Up, Please!" - A Corporate Clash

NuCom has decided to change the way it pays its hourly employees. The change involves increasing performance-based bonuses and decreasing hourly raises. The company's position is simple and justified.

A bonus-based form of compensation makes employees more cognizant of the bottom line, and leads to decreased costs, increased teamwork and higher productivity levels.

While employee communication vehicles such as meetings, articles in the company newspaper, bulletin announcements and even videotapes are used to spread the word on this change, most are laden with the typical corporate jargon and buzzwords. Employees are told things like:

> *The marketplace is changing and in order to meet this challenge we must reinvent ourselves on an ongoing basis.*

> *This new form of compensation is common in today's business world because it helps create a sense of urgency and a shared accountability for delivering added value to our customers.*

> *This is one way to bring costs into line with productivity since enhanced teamwork will allow us to achieve our future goals more cost-effectively.*

Sound familiar? Familiar indeed. These phrases certainly fit the description of corporate "old standards", right? They are very official sounding, they ring of business sophistication, and they are carefully tooled to be politically correct phrases justifying a delicate subject. But they are also devoid of any specifics about the new program, and they mistakenly assume certain areas of knowledge and perception on the part of employees.

For instance, *precisely* how will costs "…fall into line with productivity…" and *why* does a changing marketplace mean, "…we must reinvent ourselves…" and exactly what is it about a change in compensation that creates "…shared accountability…"? In fact, just what the heck is "shared accountability", anyway?

Because of these communication gaps, having heard this pitch many NuCom employees immediately become suspicious and think the worst. They feel this is just another one of what they consider greedy company moves hidden behind a facade of official sounding double-talk. Their point of view could be summarized in this way:

> *Sure the marketplace may be changing,*
> *but taking money away from employees*
> *isn't the kind of change we want!*

This new form of compensation may be common, but that just means more companies are ripping employees off as a means of getting even richer.

Here we go again with the productivity. If you want better productivity, try training us right and giving us the right tools for the job. Oh, and don't give us so much work we can't possibly do it right!

As you can see, these statements reflect suspicion and resentment, and those feelings are based in part on a lack of specific information and understanding. The result? You guessed it. The ever present Us and Them Syndrome once again begins to materialize, nurturing unrest and mistrust in the employee-company relationship.

But suppose NuCom had brought in Frank, Dick and Jane to handle the communication aspects of this delicate topic. "Brought in who?" you ask. You know Dick and Jane – the legendary first reader duo who offer an ultra-simple explanation of everything from Spot the dog to how Jane runs. And Frank? Well, you know him too. He's balanced, factual and straight up-front. He tells it like it is.

Before you laugh too loud, imagine these three are indeed on the NuCom communication team — strictly in a *symbolic* sense. In other words, they represent exactly what the company should display to its employees — honesty, simplicity, and an objective presentation of the facts.

In fact, take it one step further and imagine that acting on some good advice from Frank, Dick and Jane, a NuCom top executive calls a meeting with employees and says something like this:

> *Since we're all a part of the same company and this change is important from a management and an hourly standpoint, we all have to understand exactly what the company wants to do, why we're doing it, and how it will affect us all.*
>
> *Here are the facts:*
>
> *We're a public company, and that means above all we have to deliver a solid return to our stock holders. Whether we like it or not, that's the nature of the beast, and here's why. If we don't do it,*

investors sell our stock and we lose the critical financing we need to grow and stay healthy. We end up having to go out and borrow money, which puts us in debt — not where you'd like to be as an individual and not where we want to be as a company.

The way we figure it, there are three ways we can deliver a solid return to our investors: First, by keeping our costs as low as possible, second, by staying as competitive and profitable as we can, and third, by delivering the best quality products and services we possibly can.

Now, with that in mind, here's the logic for our bonus payment plan. We've done studies and found that more and more companies are making the changes we're proposing, and it's working for them in all three of the areas I just mentioned. They find that they are able to cut costs because employees become more focused on what it takes to run a business. They also find that employees become more tuned in to how saving money and working as a team can keep the company healthy. Employers have also discovered that employees are more likely to go the extra mile because they're actually getting a piece of the profit pie. And in most cases we've studied, employees are actually making one to three percent more money under this plan than they would have at their standard hourly rate.

And keep this in mind because it's important. Those companies that are making this system work are competitors of ours. The longer we wait to go to this system, so we, too, can cut costs and boost productivity, the more business they're stealing from us. We're actually losing money as we speak because we haven't done this.

If we all pull together and get that business back, we all make more money than we normally would have this year. Let me repeat that — more money than we normally would. But let's be straight. In today's business world we all know there are no guarantees. Everything is based on competition. So if we don't pull together, if we don't get the business, we make less money. And it's a shared responsibility because we upper managers are in the same boat as you. With less profits, we'll get less pay.

So here's where we stand today — all of us. If we don't go forward with this plan you get your standard guaranteed raises, and we get a little bit weaker as a company. I say this because we get less and less competitive every day. And eventually we either have to cut costs in some other, probably more painful way, or go out of business. That's not a threat, by the way. It's a fact. And it's a fact that this management team has decided is unacceptable.

Under the new plan we dig in and pull together, become much tougher on our competition, and we succeed together as a team, sharing in the profits.

The bottom line is this: No one is trying to line their pockets. We're trying to do what we're supposed to do as managers — make decisions that keep this company healthy and at the same time turn change into opportunity — in this case an opportunity that allows us all to increase rather than decrease our pay-checks. We think that's a pretty good deal.

The only catch is we have to work hard and work as a team. That's the only way it will work.

———

Would this Frank, Dick and Jane approach have helped?

Without question. We all know that simple facts and frank, open presentation are virtually impossible to label suspect or untrustworthy. Frankness, by its very nature, creates trust and respect. And using a simple, step-by-step, Dick and Jane approach wipes out any fear of double talk or facts "conveniently" left vague. In a word, treating controversial subjects this way gives the presenter *credibility*. And since that presenter is an executive who represents the ivory tower, the company shares in that credibility.

Granted, employees will still have arguments against the plan. Any of us who have been in business for any length of time know better than to expect magic bullets. Change the way you pay someone and insert an element of risk into it, and he or she is not going to like it. Period. But with a simple, up-front presentation of the facts, both groups can meet on the same side of the fence and approach the issue with an informed sense of trust and mutual respect. It becomes much easier and "cleaner" to deal with.

Speaking Down?

Now you may be asking yourself, "If I Dick and Jane a serious topic, will I appear to be speaking down to my employees? Will I come off as condescending?" The answer is simple. If your *tone* is condescending, yes. But simplicity by itself is not condescending at all. On the contrary, it is courteous and thoughtful to want to be absolutely sure the listener understands - especially in the case of important or controversial subjects. Wouldn't you feel grateful to a car salesman who Dick and Jane'd you through each step of a purchase?

This situation is just one of many examples. There are hundreds of ways the Us and Them Syndrome springs up in companies every day. In fact, the basic differences in perspective between senior management, middle management, first line management and hourly employees spawns the Us and Them Syndrome by its very nature. Isn't that why we tend to assume it's a given?

Well, remember this. The Us and Them Syndrome is *not* a given in your company, or any other. With Frank, Dick and Jane on your communication team, in other words a return to the philosophy of frank, clear, honest communication, it can quickly become an "Us and *Us*" attitude instead.

To see how, let's start by getting a little closer to these three legendary communicators.

Two:

The Power Trio Up Close

Following this sentence, stop reading for a moment and visualize the most important milestones you hope to achieve as a manager, and the stature you hope to see your company or department attain.

Now visualize your individual employees. How well does each one understand and support this vision of yours? Isn't it them, after all, who must actually accomplish much what you as a leader aspire to achieve? Are these elements and their importance perfectly clear to your employees today? Do you feel that your employees – including your management team if you happen to be a senior manager – are clearly tuned in to the vision? Do they respect it? Are they focusing their best collective efforts on achieving it? If so, you're sitting in a wonderful place and your success is virtually guaranteed.

And, frankly, this is a book you don't need.

If not, you're certainly not alone. And that means it's time to redefine your basic management communication style, refocusing everyone's attention to assure that your employees clearly understand four simple things:

- Your vision
- Why it is so important to achieve that vision
- How they fit into it
- How they will benefit from achieving it

Make these four items crystal clear to your workforce and the result will be a wave of concentrated energy and enthusiasm all focused and driving in the same direction — straight toward the top of the heap.

You First

Ah, but of course there's a catch! And it's a critical one. In order for this to take place, the initial enlightenment has to take place in *your* mind — not your employees'. Why? Because in order for the Frank, Dick and Jane Power Trio to fire up those you lead, your imagination has to click on and light the way. At some point you have to sit up in your chair and say:

> *Of course! I see! I understand how*
> *honest, direct communication*
> *can transform and focus the energy in*
> *this company in a way*
> *I'd never imagined!*

To help you experience that moment of clarity, let's start with a clear and simple definition of those three critical words: *Frank, Dick and Jane.*

Frank – A Definition

"Frank" is a term we all know very well, but since the objective of this book is to get back to the basics, let's "Dick and Jane" the definition, just to be sure.

Frank means:

Honest, open, direct communication —
either verbal, written

or by any other means. Other words and phrases that could be used to describe frank communication are "up-front", "no sugar coating" and "telling it like it is."

Using frank communication may sound like a no-brainer, but it can be tough to do consistently, especially when the truth is not what you'd like to share. As one very simple example, consider an employee performance review meeting in which you have to tell one of your staff that his or her work is not nearly up to par. It's not easy. This same dilemma holds true on a much broader scale when telling employees things about the company that may negatively impact them.

But if you're a frank, up front manager, it's because you know that sugar coating the truth or avoiding the negative will not solve the problem. They're smart. They know sugar coating when they hear it. They can tell when they're being manipulated. And when they sense it, their respect and trust for you go out the window.

If you do bite the bullet, however, and consistently use frank communication, you'll find that it produces something very profound:

Trust, credibility and respect

A refreshing, comforting sense among your employees that you are part of a management team that cares enough about them to be honest and up front. And it follows then that…

> …*if we're worth being told the full truth, we must certainly be important to the company and its plan for success.*

You can understand, then, why simply grasping the awesome power of frank communication is the first critical element in this book.

On the other hand, speaking, well, frankly…as powerful as our man Frank may be, he can't do it on his own. You can be as frank as you like, but if your communication is not also crystal clear and simple, you're probably wasting valuable management time.

Thus, Frank's two illustrious side-kicks – Dick and Jane:

Dick and Jane Means:

Two storybook kids we remember from childhood – well, some of us. As early readers we were dazzled by their large, colorful images on the pages of our first storybooks. Then we turned our attention to the words below each image, "See Dick run", "See Jane skip", "See Spot jump!" Simplistic? Maybe so, but Dick and Jane were there for one reason, to help us understand. And they were good. We got it. And to this day many of us still use the expression "Dick and Jane" to mean a clear, very basic method of communicating that puts ideas into plain, simple English.

Taken off the pages of our early readers and brought into the dog-eat-dog world of modern business, Dick and Jane communication means simple, active, easily understood words, phrases and examples which ensure that whatever the company's message is, it will be crystal clear to all employees.

The Communication Power-Trio

Now, take another moment and imagine the three together:

Direct, honest, ultra-simple explanations of all important company issues

And imagine a management team skilled in Frank, Dick and Jane techniques actually delivering those critical explanations in your company! What happens?

Light bulbs snap on!
Heads start to nod!
Everyone gets it!
People believe!
They see how they fit in!
They understand why they're important!

Less confusion; less frustration; less resentment!

Do they always like or agree with the information you pass on? Of course not. This is the real world, after all. But they *understand it*, and they understand how it affects them, and...

...they respect and admire you for caring
enough about them to make it clear.

Understand why I call Frank, Dick and Jane the Communication Power Trio?

Is your light bulb beginning to flicker? Showing signs of clicking on?

I hope so, because we've met the key players and we now know why they're here. That means we've arrived at the need for specifics. It's one thing to talk about being frank, clear and simple, but *how exactly is it done?* What should we do differently as managers and communicators? And how can we know we're being effective?

To find out, let's talk a little more Dick and Jane.

Three

As Simple as 1, 2, 3?

It sounds simple, right? Just be clear and direct. And it is...sort of. You see, it turns out there are a few very important action steps involved in becoming a Frank, Dick and Jane communicator. And, as you might guess, they make up a significant part of this book.

As you read through the list below, visualize. Imagine that, as a whole, these items will transform in the hands of your staff into a kind of powerful communication magnifying glass. When used collectively, these few points will turn your important thoughts, wishes and facts into crystal clear realizations in the minds of your employees, *understood exactly as you meant them.*

The Frank, Dick and Jane Communication Style
   1. Recalibrate Your Perception
   2. Focus at the Source

3. Penetrate – O. P. P. EX.
4. Present With the Structure of Simplicity
5. Try the Why Technique
6. Practice Power Empathy
7. Clarify Executive Vision

On the next few pages we'll begin with a very basic definition of each of these items. We'll then devote a chapter to each, along with an assortment of case studies that illustrate how powerful they are.

I. Recalibrate Your Perception

Think about yourself – how you perceive verbal communication. As you speak to your employees, customers and associates, how often do you think to yourself, "I want to make this message absolutely crystal clear" or, "How exactly did they interpret what I just said?"

If your answer is, "Not very often" you're like most business professionals – very busy and very comfortable that when you speak, the words that come out of your mouth are always the right ones, thus, the people you speak to always get the right message. Well, here's a wake up call – time has dulled your sense of what clear communication really is and the rapid-fire world of modern business has made it even more difficult to achieve true clarity.

To master the Frank, Dick and Jane style, you first have to understand this and become very focused on the clarity of your words. Until it becomes habit – which it does quickly – you have to continually ask yourself, "When I say this, what does he or she or they *imagine*? What is *their perception* of my message?"

This conscious attention to the importance of clarity and perception will give you a new respect for the power of your words.

2. Focus at the Source

Focus. That's number two. Why is it so important? You know why. But if your company is struggling with the Us and Them Syndrome, you and your management team aren't *using* that knowledge – or, at least not very well.

So, let's talk about it.

Think about taking a picture. If you point your camera and record an image with the lens out of focus you'll end up with a "fuzzy" negative. And from that negative you will not be able to produce a clear picture. The reason is obvious. The image you've recorded on the film was out of focus *at the source*.

The same holds true for the ideas we express in words and on paper. If we don't first clarify them in our own minds – *at the source* – we can't hope to communicate them clearly to someone else.

3. Penetrate – OPPEX

No, it's not the oil Cartels. **OPPEX** is an acronym for **Opinions, Preferences and Past Experiences**. They are the basic, built-in communication barriers that we all possess, and they have a major influence on our perception. We believe our opinions are always right. We consider our preferences flawless. And our past experiences shape virtually every word we hear or read. How to disable those barriers is the key!

4. Present With the Structure of Simplicity

Structure is a wonderful and absolutely amazing thing – especially when it comes to communicating. If you can organize and arrange your thoughts into simple, logical modules you've taken a major step in putting the Frank, Dick and Jane communication style into high gear. The light bulbs will start to click on, and the rewards you reap will be truly astounding.

5. Try the Why Technique

You may not realize it, but the simple act of telling someone why is often a pivotal element in their willingness to accept and support it – even if they don't like it or agree with you. Oddly enough, many times we tend to forget about telling employees why. Or, if we *do* tell them why, we sugar coat the facts or cloud them in vague, politically correct language – which they recognize, sooner or later.

And the result? Us and Them. So much for management credibility....

6. Practice Power Empathy

Sure, you want to get your point across. Because what you have to say is right. Right? You can see what *might* be wrong with this picture. But even if it's not. Even if you happen to be 100% right, 100% of the time, empathizing with those to whom you speak will give you an amazing insight into their feelings, and thus a great advantage in encouraging them to buy into your ideas.

7. Clarify Executive Vision

If you're running a company, department or regional group, do you have a vision of how your operation should "look" and operate? How it should evolve? Do you have a feel for the future and how working together with your staff you will achieve your business goals? If so, that's great, but it's better – *much better* – if your people understand and share that vision!

Ok, so those are a few quick snapshots of where we're headed. Now, let's get moving.

Part Two:

The Frank, Dick and Jane Communication Style

Four:

Recalibrate Your Perception

A national sales manager meets with her people to discuss quarterly results, but she continually "wanders" as she speaks.

A vice-president of public affairs explains an important media project in corporate jargon to the team that will develop it. The team leaves the meeting scratching their heads.

Three members of a well-to-do family, a husband, wife and teen-age son, are not able to clearly articulate the personal conflicts slowly eroding their relationships.

All of these statements describe situations I've been a part of as either a manager, a communication consultant or a good friend. And, as you might guess, all were extremely costly to the people involved.

> *The sales manager had to find new employment because she couldn't seem to give her people clear direction. Before she left, morale declined, sales revenues followed suit, and the Us and Them Syndrome spread like wildfire in the departments under her supervision.*

> *The vice president fell into disfavor because of this project and other communication breakdowns. He was eventually demoted. Prior to this, hundreds of thousands of dollars were wasted on misdirected efforts to launch successful campaigns.*

> *And the family? Sadly, it disintegrated over a period of several years. Frustrations first turned to resentment and eventually grew into deep seated anger and finally, hopelessness.*

Though painful, humiliating, and sometimes even devastating, when you get right down to it these are all a result of simple miscommunications – an inability to clearly express important ideas and concepts – the kind of miscommunication we're all guilty of at one time or another. And in each of these cases, had the communication been Frank, Dick and Jane, the results would surely have been very different.

Is It Complicated?

Communicating effectively is not rocket science. As we all know, it's a simple matter of speaking clearly...

- Thinking out what you want to say to achieve a specific result
- Speaking simply and clearly with a minimum of jargon or vague
  Words and phrases
- Structuring what you say in a logical, easy to follow order
- Verifying that the people you speak to understand you

Then, of course, there is the equally important, flip side of the coin:

- *Listening* carefully and openly to what others say to you

Simple stuff, right? Absolutely. Available on the bookstore shelves? In abundance. Why then do we continually suffer the Us and Them Syndrome and the many other types of communication problems that spring from poor communication? Because the real problem is not a lack of information or understanding, it's a *mind-set* – a perception that we don't need to acknowledge and apply the amazing power of simple clarity.

> *We simply don't focus on clarity*
> *when we speak and listen because*
> *we feel we don't need to.*

Damaging Assumptions

We assume that speaking clearly is a no-brainer – a matter of letting whatever words come to mind at the moment, roll off our tongues. We assume that good communication is a matter of things like tone of voice, body language and appropriate content instead of clarity. And we subconsciously assume that the people we speak to are "telepathic" enough to follow our train of thought – no matter how wide, far or often it may meander. And listening? Think about it. How often do you manage to listen – *really stop and listen* – without distractions that cloud your perception or a compulsion to get your own opinion in as quickly and forcefully as possible – or both?

And the answer to this dilemma?

> *Change how you think about personal communication. In other words, recalibrate your perception, making Frank, Dick and Jane both your communication model and basic philosophy.*

As we've said, it all starts with you. Why?

> *If you are a leader and you don't consider clear, honest communication one of your highest priorities, it will reflect in your management style. Those who follow you will question your credibility and be suspicious of your motives.*

> *On the other hand, if your people begin to sense that you take great pride in communicating frankly, simply and*

directly, the questions and suspicion will vanish, the barriers will come down and a new, positive momentum will fire up in your company like an amazing engine of success.

So how do you make that perception recalibration? Start by taking to heart the concepts we've just discussed, and making the ideas in this book your business communication framework.

Considering Your Blessings

Remember that clarity of word and thought are two of the most profound gifts we possess as human beings. And let me assure you, "profound" is the right word. Regard the words you speak and listen to as the one indisputable separator of man from all other life forms on the planet. And take great pride in your ability to reason in complex ways, perceive the subtle nuances and sensitivities of the people you speak with, and conceive powerful new ideas from the words you hear.

Most of all, remain continually aware that all of these attributes are based on one important quality – clarity…

*...the simple clarity of the communication
you give and take.*

Of course, the reason is obvious. If they don't understand you, or you don't understand them, your communication efforts, no matter how well intended, are useless.

With this new appreciation for the importance and power of the communication gift we've all been given, take some time alone now to *objectively* ask yourself a few serious questions.

- When I speak, do my employees *fully* understand me?
- Does it show in their eyes, their attitudes and their actions that they easily follow my logic?
- Could my staff be misinterpreting some of the important concepts about my vision of success and how we should execute it?
- When I conduct meetings, do my people walk away comfortable with my requests, or are there questionable silences, unsure glances and subtle head shaking?

- Are the people who work for me Frank, Dick and Jane communicators? Or have we all been too busy getting the job done to consider the powerful potential of our communication?
- Is there evidence of misunderstandings "hidden" in my operations? Productivity issues? Scheduling and coordination problems? Customer dissatisfaction? Union conflicts? An Us and Them attitude?

The objective of this soul searching exercise is critical. You must make a careful, objective analysis of how you and the people in your company interact. And, as I mentioned earlier, if the answers all come up positive, put this book aside and thank your lucky stars.

If not? Make the commitment now to bring the Frank, Dick and Jane Power Trio into your company or operation. View it in two ways:

- **As a company or departmental standard:** A way of communicating that all management employees will be expected to adhere to, and…

- **As a basic communication philosophy:**
  A conceptual belief that open, honest and simple communication is a basic requirement for your company's future success.

Decide, in no uncertain terms, that as of this moment no employee will ever again be given instructions, a performance review or be delegated a task without being 100% clear on what it is, what it involves and how it fits into the big picture.

Are you in?

Congratulations, you've made the critical leap!

F D & J Bullet Plate

Recalibrate Your Perception

✓ Acknowledge the profound importance and power of clear communication
✓ Objectively think through how you and your people communicate
✓ Commit to Frank, Dick and Jane as a company or departmental standard and a basic communication philosophy

Five:

Focus at the Source

During a typical business day many of us blurt out more than our share of vague, poorly focused thoughts and meandering streams of idea fragments. When these involve unimportant conversations, the consequences are minor. If someone is sent out for a veggie pizza and brings back Italian sausage, a little heartburn will probably be the worst of it.

But as we all know, there are many times when much, *much* more is at stake. The following is a true example...

Case Study - A Costly Conversation

Bill Simpson is a successful financial planner for a fortune 500 company. On one Friday afternoon he is in his typical "fly by the seat of his pants" mode. He is headed first down the hall to get some advice from an attorney friend, then back to his office briefly to pick up some paperwork, and a short time later he's scheduled to speak across town at a business meeting. Before leaving for the meeting, he needs several pieces of information from a client, Dan Miller, and his wife, Carol. He needs:

> Dan's investment portfolio for the current year. Dan's W-2 income for the current year, and the same information from Carol.

Bill decides to have his secretary get this information while he's down the hall visiting the attorney so he can pick it up on his way out of the office. He also wants Dan and Carol to be aware that he is planning to anonymously present the couple's financial "profile" in the meeting as a model for proper investment strategies. He has decided to do this for two reasons. First, he does indeed feel their profile is an excellent example of sound investment principles, and second, he knows he needs to get in a few points with these two clients since they've been somewhat unsatisfied with his availability. As good as he is at numbers, Bill is not so great at returning calls. He's always too busy.

As he is leaving for the attorney's office, he turns to his secretary and says:

> *I need the Miller's investments and W-2 income. Both of 'em. And call Dan and Carol. Let 'em know. I'll pick 'em up on my way out. I'll present them in the meeting this afternoon.*

As he rushes out the door, his secretary (who is in the middle of several other chores and frantically scribbling notes) tries to make sense of what she's just heard. After a few moments she's decided she's gotten it right. She pulls the investment files on Dan and Carol and writes down their income. She then quickly checks her notes again, dials the Millers, and in a bubbly tone says...

> *Guess what! Bill is on his way to pick you and Carol up. He's presenting your investments and your income in a meeting this afternoon.*

Dan is floored. He has been trying to reach Bill for the past week to discuss his portfolio, but Bill has not returned his calls. Now, out of the blue, comes this bizarre request. Present his financials to a group of strangers?

So, he blows up and decides this is the final straw. He's leaving the firm. In fact, he tells the secretary he's coming down immediately to sign the papers and transfer his money to another firm.

Dan and Carol, by the way, are a $4,000,000 account!

Shortly after the now distraught secretary hangs up, Bill returns from the attorney's office ready to pick up the papers and leave. After being told what has happened, he immediately tries to call Dan and Carol. Carol answers, saying she's sorry but Dan is furious and he's on his way down to cancel their accounts. Bill knows it will take Dan thirty minutes to reach his office. Bill was due to start his presentation in the meeting in *twenty* minutes.

Deciding he has no choice but to wait for Dan and try to save the account, Bill hands his dumbfounded assistant a pack of roughly scribbled notes, quickly briefs her, and sends her to the meeting to speak in his place.

Thirty minutes later, Bill gives it his best shot, but Dan and Carol leave the firm. Meanwhile, across town the presentation has been a disaster because Bill's assistant is totally unprepared... More lost business.

Bizarre, indeed, but as I said, a true story. And the losses here run deeper than is first evident. The loss of a nine million dollar account is bad enough, but what about the business Bill might have gleaned from his presentation at the meeting? And how about future business he will lose as a result of Dan and Carol's poor reviews of his customer handling and communication skills?

This little fiasco has also strengthened the Us and Them Syndrome in Bill's office. The assistant was upset, since she'd been thrown (once again) into an embarrassing, no-win situation, and the secretary became even more hesitant to take Bill's instructions at face value. And the larger problem? This wasn't the first time. Bill is a very effective financial planner, but he's also a shoot from the hip communicator. He rarely thinks out what he wants to say. As a result, the Us and Them Syndrome is deeply entrenched in his business. His employees resent and mistrust him, and though Bill doesn't realize it, this is costing him in many ways.

You get the point. Speaking about important issues without forethought, can and often does, have *exponential* negative impact.

The Solution

Avoiding this kind of crash and burn incident involves a three-step process, which we'll cover in this and the next two chapters. The first step is amazingly simple:

Focus Your Message
Take the time to think out what you want to say and be sure you've got it right.

If Bill had simply taken a deep breath, thought for a moment and made the following Frank, Dick and Jane statement, none of the losses he suffered would have occurred:

> *Anne, I'm on my way down the hall for a few minutes to see Jack. While I'm gone, Call Dan and Carol Miller and let them know I'd like to present their investment profile as an example of excellent investment principles in the talk I'm giving this afternoon. Be sure to tell them*

I'll keep it anonymous, of course. If they give permission, pull their W-2 income and investment portfolio. I'll pick up the folders on my way out to the meeting.

Did Bill know this? Of course he did. Do you and I know it? Certainly. But did Bill *think* about it? Absolutely not. Clear communication was the last thing on his mind. Would greater appreciation for clarity and an extra *ten or twenty seconds* have allowed him to focus his message at the source and avoid this problem? Absolutely.

Focus at the What?

So what *exactly* do I mean by "focus at the *source*"? Remember the analogy we mentioned a few chapters back? You'd be wise to commit it to memory:

If you take a picture with your camera and the lens is out of focus, the image recorded the negative will be fuzzy. A fuzzy negative cannot be fixed. People will view the print made from it as poorly shot. And if it's too far out of focus, it may not even be recognizable! The same holds true for the ideas in your mind and the words you speak. If they are out of focus at the source – in your mind – they can't possibly be communicated clearly to someone else clearly.

So, how do you gain this focus? Using two simple skills:

Analysis and Objectivity

Analysis – Think About It

Here's a simple example. Imagine you're a middle manager and one of your front-line supervisors, John Doe, shows up half an hour late to work for the fourth time this month. As he walks past your office door, if you're irritated and you don't stop to think about what you're about to say, it may just pop out something like,

So, John, do you ever plan to show up on time?

This will certainly offend John and support the Us and Them Syndrome, so if that's your intent, mission accomplished. But if you'd rather have John be punctual and understand why being late is detrimental to his career, you might want to take just a minute to think about that and what you could say to bring it about. In doing so, you'd probably come up with the idea that if you could Frank, Dick and Jane this employee on the true impact of being late, you might just get a more positive outcome.

In that case, you would probably ask him to sit down, and in a calm, level, Frank, Dick and Jane tone of voice, say something like:

> *John, I owe it to you to be truthful. As far as I'm concerned, being late four times in one month is careless, inconsiderate and it shows very bad judgment.*
>
> *I don't like saying this to you and I don't want to form a negative image of you, but that's what's happening. Can you please be here on time – consistently?*

Will he be on time the next day? If he has any work ethic at all, you bet he will (if not, he shouldn't be working for you in the first place). And you can be assured he also understands why it's so important. Oh, and very important – he'll *respect* you for being frank, though he might not admit it.

Objectivity – Limit Distortion

Now, I said there were two aspects to gaining focus. The second one was objectivity. In this situation, as in many employee supervisor interactions, emotions can distort the clarity of a message and blow things out of proportion.

In the first interaction with John, the comment, "John, do you ever plan to come to work on time?" would probably have been delivered with a terse or resentful tone. So the comment had two strikes against it. Not only was it out of focus at the source, it also displayed a subjective, abrasive tone. In the second case, however, if the comments were spoken with a calm level tone, not only was the message very clear, it was also very objective and unemotional. A great Frank, Dick and Jane combination.

Now ask yourself another question. Remembering that this was one relatively minor example, if this type of interaction is going on constantly in your company on a much broader scale, if employees are being communicated to "on the fly" with unfocused communication multiple times every day, could the Us and Them Syndrome result? And if that changed – if they suddenly experienced communication from your staff in a thoughtful focused way, would it tend to eliminate the Us and Them Syndrome?

The answer is obvious.

But it may raise another question in your mind...

Do I have to stop, think and carefully focus every word I say?

The answer is no. If you did, that hustle-bustle world of fire-fights and constantly shifting priorities would gobble you up before you got a word out edgewise. What you do have to do, however, is decide that *focusing your message* is a critical first step in clarifying your verbal communications, and therefore you're going to make it a priority and consciously work it into your communication style. The key words here are "priority" and "consciously". If you do these two things and nothing more, you'll be amazed to find that before you know it, it will just come naturally.

And don't forget there are many times your communication isn't "on the spot". In fact, in lots of cases you have plenty of time to think out what you want to say:

- Before meetings with your bosses and customers
- Before meetings with your employees, peers, clients and vendors

- Before you speak in front of groups
- Before you make sales pitches

So? The first simple step to a Frank, Dick and Jane communication style?

Focus at the Source

Just stop and think about it! Make focusing and deciding on a preferred outcome a conscious priority.

Assuming you're well on the road to recalibrating you perception and you're now clear on how to focus at the source, you've taken two very important, very positive steps.

But does this make you a Frank, Dick and Jane communicator?

Not so fast....

F. D. & J. Bullet Pack

Focus Your Message at the Source

✓ Clarify: what you plan to say in your
   own mind
✓ Analysis: Think out what you want to
   communicate and the outcome you
   want
✓ Objectivity: communicate without the
   distortion of emotion

Six:

Penetrate OPPEX

Ever say one thing to a person then find out later they heard something completely different? Welcome to the world of personal barriers. We all have them – internal filters that cause us to interpret what people tell us according to our own set of parameters. I call them OPPEX, short for: **opinions, preferences and past experiences**. They are personal barriers because they block true clarity in communication. They can actually transform the meaning of our words and they are one of the toughest perpetuators of the Us and Them Syndrome that we face.

Consider a simple example.

As a car salesman talks to a customer about a new car, he says. . .

> *And another great thing - this beauty won't need any trips to the shop for 5 years!*

He may feel he's been clear with his message, but he's mistaken. That's because his customer's interpretation of the words "…won't need any trips to the shop for 5 years!" will be filtered and changed by their personal barriers.

For instance, let's suppose the customer happens to be a salesman himself, one who drives thousands of miles per year in a large territory. He might interpret the statement "…won't need any trips to the shop…" to mean he won't get stranded by the side of the road, as he has several times, and have to be towed to the nearest garage.

Or, if he's a donut shop owner whose last car was hard to start on cold mornings, he'll probably remember how he'd have to call AAA every few months to charge the battery. He may then interpret the salesman's statement to mean that no matter how thick the frost, ice or snow, that engine will turn over. No more AAA – for 5 years!

Or, if it's a woman who's suspicious of car salesman (who isn't), she may feel the salesman is feeding her a line of baloney – but one that she's not quite clear on. After all, "….no trips to the shop for 5 _years!_"? Really?

These are all legitimate personal interpretations of what the salesman said. As you can see they are all different and all created by each individual's personal barriers – opinions, preferences and past experiences. But what if the salesman had said what he *really meant* by "…won't need any trips to the shop for year!"

> *And, you'll be happy to know that this car is guaranteed to run for 5 years or 50,000 miles before you'll have to pay for any factory service.*

Had this been the case, regardless of the customers' OPPEX, they would have had no choice. They would have understood *exactly* what the salesman was saying, on his terms. "…won't need any trips to the shop for 5 years!" really meant *free factory service for five years – guaranteed*. The salesman's clarity factor in this case would have been very high. Why? He penetrated his customers' personal barriers. He expressed himself in a way that did not allow the customers to distort his message.

This little story points up the fact that penetrating a person's OPPEX is a matter of focusing on the *clarity* and *simplicity* of your words, so that what you say is...

> ...*precise, detailed and, whenever possible, stated with visual qualities.*

In your company, penetrating OPPEX could apply to any number of very important topics – productivity analysis, an employee's assignment, a performance review, personal objectives discussions, company goals, revenue targets, sales quotas and, of course, the list could go on...and on!

Here are a few Frank, Dick and Jane basics that can help you put this important step into action.

Use Precise, Visual Language

That means using active verbs and nouns. In other words...

> **Don't say**: *Adherence to the budget figures we've set is questionable.*
> **Instead say:** *We can't live with this budget.*

> **Don't say**: *Sales are showing signs of accelerating weakness.*

Instead say: *Sales revenues took a 20 percent nose dive this month.*

Don't say: *The program has produced impressive results.*
Instead say: *The incentive program has returned a 12 percent increase, boosted employee morale and put us in the black for the first time in six months!*

Don't say: *Our competitive challenges are multiplying annually.*
Instead say: *Every year we face more competitors.*

Don't say: *We have to acknowledge that business is becoming increasingly difficult.*
Instead say: *Let's face it, business is getting tougher every year!*

See the difference? Active and precise word choices tend to convey clear, dynamic images while passive and vague language conveys cloudy, partially formed images.

Avoid Corporate Mumbo-Jumbo

Nothing is better at *strengthening* OPPEX than blurring the meaning of your message with corporate-speak.

To illustrate that point, let's take a short detour for an example with a bit of a chuckle.

For several years I taught corporate media production at a film school in New England. In one of my classes each student was required to direct a short scene using actors. I wrote the scripts for these scenes, which were typically one to two pages in length. One year I decided it might be fun to spoof the corporate boardroom with the following scene:

THE MEETING
FADE IN:
INT. EXECUTIVE
BOARDROOM - DAY

Two high level corporate executives are seated in a large plush office. One is the CEO. The other is an Executive VP. They are engaged in a serious, very important strategic meeting. The VP stays seated during most of the conversation. The CEO gets to his feet soon after the conversations begins and paces, thinking over each point made in the discussion.

CEO

Are they aware of our strategy?

EXEC.VP

The vertical integration plan?

CEO

Right. The revised version sanctioned by the board.

EXEC, VP

Sure. The efficiency numbers alluding to our market posture are a part of the first section. Hell, it's obvious.

CEO

Post-quarter numbers?

EXEC.VP

Exactly. Annualized to include the relative shares of each capital driven element...by weighted percentages, of course.

CEO

Those outlined in the General Plan, endorsed section on diverse investment in human resources as opposed to technical micro-elements?

EXEC.VP

Right on. Section five of the appended output of our quality caliber V-Code input data. The centralized input of invested members versus attending elements held at account level.

CEO

Excellent! So we'll have it both ways! The ramification listings inserted in vertically integrating the relative weightings will contrast the calculated indices based on consortium level derivatives brought forward from other applications!

EXEC.VP

Which...if projected three fiscal quarters into the future, and factored in with running M-load indices from 09 through 12 respectively, suggest that the deregulation strategy put forth centralized consortium level – even with non-elemental infusion runs – can bolster vertical enticement, subject, of course, to a series of policies...

(a sudden, depressing realization)

...deemed...functionally...*essential!*

CEO
(also depressed)
The *catch*!... Of course!

EXEC.VP
Damn! So what do we do?....

CEO
We go over it again – this time in detail....

FADE OUT:

When I gave this script to the student who would direct it, he didn't understand. "But it's just a bunch of gobbledygook," he said.

"That's exactly right," I responded. "Isn't that *funny* to you?"

He gave me a puzzled look.

"Think about it," I said. "The audience is watching these two polished, time-hardened executives strategizing in a corporate board room. But as they start to talk, it occurs to the audience that what's being said is kind of muddled. As the scene continues, it becomes a little more obvious that something is screwy. Audience members begin to think to themselves... 'these two are *really* talking corporate mumbo-jumbo.' Finally, it dawns on them that as lean and mean and nasty as the pair may look, these two guys aren't really saying *anything at all*! We've tricked our audience, pulled one over on them by putting a straight face on the typical corporate stereotype. And when they realize that, they start laughing.

Well, the student wasn't convinced my idea would work, but he did go along with it. He directed the scene deadpan straight. The two actors never cracked a smile or hinted in any way that they weren't one hundred percent serious. And when we edited the piece and showed it, the work paid off. The audience roared.

Now, as I said, this little story has a humorous slant, but let's be serious. Business communications do have a reputation of being glossed over and weighted down with "official" mumbo-jumbo. And to a large degree, that reputation has been earned. The phrase "weighted down" should actually be "lightened up", by the way, because when something you're trying to communicate becomes more trouble to understand than it appears to be worth, the ideas just sort of glide away into the ether and leave the audience in a trance.

Or, even worse, if the topic happens to be controversial to your employees – for instance how they are paid or what they will be responsible for or the hours they will work, or some new program that requires significant change – well, you can guess the end result: suspicion, resentment, possible disobedience and sometimes plain old anger – the Us and Them Syndrome.

Use Those Analogies

We all know that analogies are parallels drawn between an idea being expressed and some person, place or thing that helps make the point. Connecting the two ideas usually creates a common *visual* reference between the speaker and the listener or reader. When it comes to making things clear and vivid, analogies are a great communication tool.

The following are a few common business ideas that might normally be expressed in straight, non-visual terms. Also listed are some analogies that give them visual qualities.

Straight Version	Analogy
Our customer service plan is weak and lethargic.	*This customer service plan is inching along like a snail in a coma*
Our employee motivation program is gaining momentum every day.	*Our employee motivation program is rolling through this company like a tidal wave of positive energy.*
This was the most productive sales campaign we've ever undertaken.	*This started as a sales campaign and turned into a truckload of profits headed straight for the bank!*

Using Analogies as a General Theme

You may have noticed that the examples we just focused on are limited to single phrases or ideas. Analogies can also be used to highlight a *general theme*. For instance, I once saw a television interview in which a famous politician referred to "building bridges" between the haves and have nots in our society. He used the visual image of a bridge as a general theme and talked eloquently about crossing it, sharing ideas, educational opportunities, job opportunities, and so on. He finished his comments by saying that if we could only meet each other half way, at the middle of the bridge, maybe then we'd be more apt to share with those on the other side. His use of the bridge as a general theme gave his comments a visual quality that tied them together powerfully for the millions of viewers watching.

Themes using powerful analogies can be very effective when it's time for one of those motivational employee presentations. There is danger, however. Getting corny or "sugar coated" is a sure-fire downer. Outlandish or grandiose analogies that are meant to disguise some controversial issue or manipulate employees will almost certainly backfire on the spot.

Fill in the Blanks

One of the worst offenses you can make when trying to communicate clearly is leaving out information. But it's surprising how many of us do it and how often. In fact, breaking the logically structured flow of information may be the most frequent mistake we make as communicators – and one of the most detrimental.

Many times, especially when we're in a rush, we assume that if we thought it, we said it. Unfortunately, that's often not the case. And leaving blanks in the stream of information you're trying to make clear is disorienting, jarring, and like poor structure, it has the effect of stopping the listener's thought process so he or she can figure out what's being said!

The solution, of course, is closely related to our first Frank, Dick and Jane step. Simply think out what you plan to say. In doing so, you'll be sure all the blanks have been filled in.

Ask for Feedback

If you don't sense a good, clean connection between you and your listeners (and remember, as a Frank, Dick and Jane communicator you're intent on this), simply ask if you got through. Say something like, "See what I mean?" or "Make sense?" or "Am I being perfectly clear?" Then look for those click on light bulbs that signal understanding.

When All Else Fails, Restate

Finally, if you have to, say it again in a different way. You can start with a phrase like, "What I meant is this..." or "In other words..." or "So what I'm saying is…" It's a good idea to follow up a restatement with another request for feedback, like, "So now are we perfectly clear on that?"

F D & J Bullet Plate

Penetrate OPPEX

- ✓ Communication is distorted by individual preferences, opinions and past experiences
- ✓ To limit this distortion, use precise visual language
- ✓ Eliminate corporate mumbo-jumbo
- ✓ Use analogies
- ✓ Fill in the blanks
- ✓ Ask for feedback
- ✓ Restate when necessary

Seven:

Tell 'Em!

Consider what's happened so far.

You've decided to make Frank, Dick and Jane a solid commitment, and you've learned the importance of clearly focusing and stating your message in a way that penetrates OPPEX. Next? You have to get it out there – *say the words* clearly and simply. Sounds easy enough, but it's a little more involved than you think. Why? Consider the business world you live in. The things you talk about can often be complicated and clouded with facets, verbiage and jargon that may be very familiar to you and your team, but foreign and thus very "murky" and "suspicious" to your people...and even more so to their people.

Perfect fodder for the Us and Them Syndrome.

One of the most important ways to avoid these barriers is to be very orderly with the *structure* of what you say. In other words…

Practice the structure of simplicity

To clarify, let's start with another example.

Film directors pay close attention to something called screen direction. It's a term that refers to the direction of objects moving on screen. It might be actors, a bus or train or a car – anything that we as viewers focus on. The reason directors are so concerned with screen direction is that if it's not carefully planned during shooting, it can result in something film people call a "screen direction reversal."

Here's a example. If a train is filmed leaving a station and it's moving from the left side of the TV screen toward the right, we viewers subconsciously assume that its destination is somewhere in that direction – toward the right. So if in the next shot the train happens to be moving in the *opposite* direction – from the right to the left – it's momentarily disorienting to us. For an instant we think the train has turned around and is headed back to the station!

Speaking to one person or a group of people poses similar dangers with words. We orient listeners by what we say when we establish topics, and if we don't follow through and keep our ideas "moving in the same direction," our listeners undergo a kind of verbal communication reversal of screen direction. They become confused for a moment and then have to catch up to our train of thought – which has moved ahead by then and perhaps deprived them of critical information.

If this continues to happen, the result is very common – a sort of partial or "surface" understanding in which the general ideas may be conveyed, but much of the detail is lost – the kind of thing Frank, Dick and Jane would never stand for.

But when a message is clearly focused at the source and then placed in a simple, logical structure, your listeners will remain in perfect sync with you and clearly follow your train of thought – no matter which way it may have been going when it left the station. And that means rich, crystal clear Frank, Dick and Jane understanding.

So how is perfect sync achieved?

The Legendary "Tell 'em" Technique

Ever heard the term "Tell 'em you're goanna tell 'em, tell 'em; and tell 'em you told 'em"? It's a traditional three-step training technique that originated many years ago. It's also a time proven winner when it comes to conveying information clearly. It's very basic, admittedly simplistic, but also extremely effective.

Here's how it works.

> ***"Tell 'em you're gonna tell 'em"*** *means you should first give your listeners a brief general introduction containing the main topics you plan to cover.*

> ***"Tell 'em"*** *means you then deliver the main body of your message by elaborating on those same topics in the same order — but, of course, in full detail. And finally...*

> ***"Tell 'em you told 'em"*** *means you should close with a simple summary that generally reiterates what you'd like people to leave with in their minds.*

Here's a very much abbreviated example.

You are chairing a meeting to achieve three important objectives: create a focus on costs, review your staff's specific cost-cutting measures and develop a plan to communicate those measures to your employees. You've taken the time to focus at the source and now, using the "Tell 'em..." method, here is an abbreviated version of what you might say:

("Tell 'em you're gonna tell "em")

Thanks for coming today. We've got some very important topics to cover. First, I want to go over our expenses for the last quarter, then I'd like to cover the cost-cutting measures you've each come up with, and finally I want to talk about how we plan to communicate all this to our employees. (When you are sure everyone is clear on these three key topic points, you continue with...)

("Tell 'em")

So let's start with expenses. Bill, you can take us through each cost category on the P&L statement for the quarter. And as we go, I'd like to discuss each one in detail...

(When all details regarding costs on the P& L have been covered, you would say...)

Okay, so we all have a clear picture of what our costs have been this quarter, now let's move on to cost-cutting measures. We'll start with Jim and move around the table. I'd like all of you to take your time and be very specific about the plans you've come up with.

(This would provide elaboration on topic number two, cost cutting measures. Following the round-table discussion, you might say....)

Good, now let's cover how we plan to make our actions clear to employees. And I hope to focus here on also telling them why these measures are important.

(After this final point had been elaborated on you could close with...)

("Tell 'em you told 'em")

Well, I'd say this has been very productive. We've got a clear focus on our costs, we've got specific plans on how to trim them significantly, and we have a plan to tell our employees exactly what we're doing and why. The next step is action. I'm very clear on all this, but I want to be sure you are, too – everyone.
Any questions or concerns on what we've covered?

What you just said was very simple, but extremely effective. You told them what you were going to say, you then discussed those issues in the same order but in greater detail, and finally you summarized and asked for confirmation that everyone understood.

Simple, direct, crystal clear! Everyone leaves the meeting on the same page, there are no questions or unsettling issues left unresolved and action steps can begin at once. A perfect Us and Them Syndrome buster.

F D & J Bullet Plate

Practice the Structure of Simplicity

✓ Carefully structure what you say using a logical flow

✓ Use the "Tell 'em" technique

Eight:

Try the Why Technique

I began my career working for a large telecommunications corporation (at that time known as "the phone company"). In those early years I was a Telephone Repair Technician. I spent a good deal of my time working on what were called Special Inspects, which meant trying to solve intermittent problems for very irate customers. Most of my coworkers wouldn't have had my job for the world, but I loved it. Why? I had a secret. I discovered early on that because customers had no idea how a telephone worked, clearly and simply explaining basic telephony — relating, of course, to *why* their phone was acting up — often defused even the angriest customers.

It was my track record with these "kid glove" customers that called attention to my communication skills and soon opened the door to my first management position. Over the years I've used this Why Technique countless times in a variety of customer, employee, executive and personal interactions. Though the situations were all different, the results are almost always the same – positive cooperation.

The power of the Why Technique at eliminating the Us and Them Syndrome, is virtually amazing. That makes it a natural part of the Frank, Dick and Jane communication style, so let's take a closer look at it.

Why is "Why" So Powerful?

When we're told why things aren't as we expect, we *understand a bigger picture,* and that understanding has a great calming affect – it's that simple. On the other hand, when we're *not* told why, we feel uneasy, defensive, even angry, simply because whatever it is we're concerned about remains an unknown. In some cases, we also become suspicious that the truth is being hidden from us. And in business, suspicions are the high power accelerators of the Us and Them Syndrome.

To understand why, read the following sentences. Imagine they are being told to you by business or academic professionals, and in each case they are the only explanation you're given:

Your car needs $1,200 worth of work.

You're not going to make any return on your investment this year.

Our company is downsizing and your department is at risk.

Your child got suspended from school today.

Your gas bill is about to go up 10 percent.

Your performance isn't up to par.

How would being the recipient of these sentences make you feel? Uneasy? Defensive? Angry? Suspicious? Exactly.

- $1,200 for a little car work? You can't be serious!
- No investment income? *No way!*

- Downsizing! Oh, no. Am I about to be homeless?
- Suspended! What in the world has that boy done now?
- Ten percent more for gas each month? Outrageous!
- What have I done now?

Obviously, there's no way to make these kinds of statements into *good* news. And doesn't that make them very much like the kinds of bad news managers hate to give employees? The kinds of news typically sugar coated with corporate mumbo-jumbo or avoided altogether? You got it. And that's why they're at the top of the list of Us and Them Syndrome perpetuators.

Now read the following Why Technique versions of the same statements and see if they're a little easier to take:

Your car needs $1,200 worth of work.

The seals in your transmission have hardened with time and are now leaking. If we don't replace them your transmission will eventually go out and *that's a $3,500 bill. In order to make the replacements, we need to disconnect the transmission from the drive train and dismantle it. The job will take about nine hours. I know $1,200 is a lot of money, but in the long run it's well worth it.*

You're not going to make any return on your investment this year.

The stock market has gone through several corrections this year and it hasn't recovered yet. Corrections of this kind are very normal in a healthy stock market, so we feel there's no need to be too concerned.

We're hoping for a significant upswing in the first quarter of next year.

Our company is downsizing and your department is at risk.

More and more small competitors are stealing our customers. Because they're small, they can also undercut our prices and act more quickly than we can. We have to shrink to be competitive. We have no other choice if we want to stay in business, and we've trimmed in every other area we can possibly manage. We're doing everything we can to preserve jobs, but I wanted to be honest and tell you where things stand.

Your child got suspended from school today.

Your daughter was caught for the third time cheating on exams. We feel she will only learn a strong lesson by taking responsibility for her actions.

We also feel it's unfair to the students who are studying diligently to make high scores. She can return to school next week and we think the experience will get her back on the right track.

Your gas bill is about to go up 10 percent.

You may not realize it, but we have to buy the gas we provide to your home. Natural gas prices have skyrocketed over the past decade and we've done everything we possibly can to keep from raising our rates. As much as we dislike it, we have no choice but to pass this increase on to our customers.

Your performance isn't up to par.
It's your productivity that concerns me and it seems to be due to a lack of effort and basic job skills. Other employees in your position have productivity factors averaging ten percent more efficient than yours. I feel with some effort on your part, some additional training and supervisory support, you can bring your factor into line within the next few months.

Better? A little less distressing? As I said, the Why Technique can't make bad news into good, but it can definitely reduce the uneasiness and anger that often accompanies it – and increase the *clarity* that diffuses suspicion and resentment.

To deal a crippling blow to the Us and Them Syndrome in your operation, try using the Why Technique in situations like…

- When explaining company changes
- When explaining departmental changes
- In employee performance review meetings
- In conversations with customers about service outages
- In conversations with customers about product deficiencies
- When giving bad news to the boss

Why is Not an Excuse

Keep in mind that when explaining a mistake to your boss, customers or your employees, the Why Technique should not be used as an excuse. As we all know, the best course of action when we've goofed is simply to own up to our mistake, whether we're speaking up or down the ladder. But explaining *why* the mistake was made can have two positive effects. First, it informs your employees of the big picture, which has that calming effect I mentioned. Second, when explaining a mistake to your boss, if your *why* leads to a positive solution to the problem it shows you have a clear understanding of what went wrong and a way to correct it. Few things are more irritating to a boss or customer than someone who's made a mistake but won't own up to it or just doesn't "get it."

On the Home Front

Although we're talking mostly business, keep in mind that the Why Technique and just about all the other techniques we're exploring in this book can also be very effective in your personal life. For instance, your children will be much more apt to go along with your curfews, restrictions and other rules if they understand why you've imposed them. The same holds true for your spouse when you don't agree on some personal matter or event.

Don't Be Afraid to Ask for It

If you happen to be on the receiving end of murky or vague communication, don't be afraid to ask for the Why. This can be difficult in meetings when "the big guy" is speaking and not being clear. Adding to the discomfort is the probability that everyone else in the room is nodding their heads and mumbling things like "absolutely", "sure thing," and "right on".

Don't let that phase you. If you don't get it, *ask*. The key is to use tact, but don't settle for a tip of the iceberg understanding.

Remember, if you are not clear on it,
you can't make it clear to others.
Enter the Us and Them Syndrome!

And getting back to your personal life, in sales situations – especially high dollar ones – you should *insist* on the Why. In fact, you should *insist* on getting the Frank, Dick and Jane on things like approving and signing any contract, why you're paying a certain price, and any part of a bill or agreement that isn't perfectly clear. If the person you're dealing with isn't forthcoming with the "why", or if they make you feel uncomfortable or stupid for asking, chances are you're better off spending your money in a more open sales environment.

The Bottom Line - "Why"

When you tell people why, you place them at ease simply by removing the unknown. It's obvious how invaluable this can be in employee interactions – especially when the Us and Them Syndrome is undermining your efforts. You also open the door to logical, constructive input from those who surround you – your employees and family members in particular – because they will be much more likely to cooperate when *you've* taken the time to make them understand…why!

F D & J Bullet Plate

Try the Why Technique

✓ Always explain *why* – whether the news is good or bad
✓ Don't use Why as an excuse, but do use it to clarify
✓ Don't be afraid to ask for the why – on the job and in your personal life

Nine:

Power Empathy

Are you a good listener? Do you take the time to empathize with your employees, customers and clients? If your response is yes, but with a slight twinge of hesitation, answer these questions...honestly:

> *When employees come to me for help, do I often think to myself, "Not another problem. I don't have time for this!"*

> *When customers complain to me about products or services, do I sometimes think, "Haven't we done enough for you? Give me a break already!"*

> *When clients ask for a little extra "TLC" from me, do I grumble in my mind, "Oh, no, here we go again! What this time?"*

Sound familiar? If so, you can take comfort in the knowledge that you're not alone. In fact, you're one of the crowd. Whether we choose to admit it or not, many of us often feel too pressured and harried to empathize with our customers, employees, bosses — and loved ones!

Now, before you go and get too comfortable in that crowd, here's another thought to keep in mind...

> One of the most important skills you possess as a human being, and possibly the most critical aspect of the Frank, Dick and Jane communication style, is the ability to listen with empathy.

Remember also, that we all make an effort to listen, but the important thing is *how* we listen.

What Is Listening With Empathy?

Listening with empathy means listening to more than just the "tip of the iceberg." In today's hustle-bustle world of business, more often than not we simply skim the surface, or focus on the "tip" because we're too frazzled doing mental gymnastics with the many other issues we face. And if we're not too distracted by other "priorities," we often focus on *our response* to the speaker before we truly understand what's being said. In other words, we're thinking more about getting our own two cents in than what the other person is trying to convey to us!

While this "tip of the iceberg" listening may get us through many verbal exchanges with short term success, the price we pay in the long run is huge. Why? Because listening without empathy discourages understanding, depth and true human connection.

For instance, when one of your employees shakes his head and says:

> *"I just can't make our deadline; things have just been too crazy!"*

A "tip of the iceberg" understanding of this statement might unfold in your mind something like:

> *"Okay, so things are crazy. What else is new. They're crazy for me, too!"*

Or you may be *subconsciously* saying something like this to yourself:

> *"He's looking for an out. It's important to maintain control. How should I respond? Should I be forceful? Angry? Disappointed?"*

Empathizing with this employee, however, would produce a deeper and more accurate understanding in your mind – something like this:

> *"I can see he's upset and he seems sincere. What exactly does 'crazy' mean to him? Why, specifically, isn't he going to make the deadline? Training issues? Scheduling? Personal problems? What kinds of negatives could he be dealing with that I might be able to help solve so we can pull this off? We'll discuss this and see if we can get to the bottom of it."*

See the difference? The first version creates a very brief and shallow interpretation of the employee's words (the tip of the iceberg). The second version focuses more on a response – getting your two cents in. The third interpretation focuses clearly on what the employee is saying. It's an attempt to *empathize* in order to gain a deeper and more precise understanding of how he feels and why.

It's only from this type of listening – with empathy – that truly meaningful solutions are born and managerial power springs. And that makes it what you might refer to as "the other side of the coin" in the Frank, Dick and Jane communication style. In other words, *listening with empathy* fulfills your obligation as a manager to not just express your own ideas clearly, but also to openly consider and understand the ideas others have to offer.

So How Exactly is It Done?

As important and, unfortunately, rare as listening with empathy may be, it's simply a matter of using three easy to remember steps:

Let Down Your Own OPPEX Communication Barriers

As we've said, we *all* have them, like it or not. Some managers are very opinionated while others tend not to trust what they hear based on some past experience. Still others simply feel they're the voice of authority, or subconsciously assume that deadlines and "fire-fights" are more important than the ideas of the people around them.

In order to listen with empathy you must first *consciously* discipline yourself to put these barriers aside for the moment, and open up to the possibility that you may be about to hear something important – maybe even valuable.

Attempt To View the Problem From the Other Person's Point of View

Once you've opened up and made a connection with the speaker, follow the old adage and "place yourself in his or her shoes." Attempt to see and *feel* the issue as the person speaking does. How does he or she *really* feel about it? If it's a customer, is she genuinely upset about what's happened? If it's an employee, is he sincere about his complaint? If it's a client, does he seem under pressure and in dire need of your assistance? And in each of these cases, *why?*

The trick, as I said, is to *consciously* make this "leap" of empathy, rather than just assume it will happen automatically – because chances are, if you don't help it along, it *won't* happen!

Do Unto Others...

With those two steps accomplished, you'll find yourself at a very old bit of biblical wisdom. "Do unto others as you would have them do unto you." Good book aside, strictly on a business or personal level, this statement is as true today as the day it was written. Treating people the way you would like or expect to be treated is the simplest, sure-fire way to display genuine empathy, and derail the Us and Them Syndrome.

This type of listening creates true human connections between you and your employees, customers, clients and loved ones. In essence, you become sensitive to their feelings. You show them you care about what they have to tell you. You read between the lines and see below the surface, thus you *understand* the ideas they're attempting to get across.

Does Empathizing Mean I Have To Agree?

Not at all. In the case of the employee mentioned earlier, you may know that he or she tends to "encounter" problems on every project you assign. If that's the case, you may *disagree* with the statement because you know that "…it's just been too crazy" is simply a standard excuse for this individual. Even assuming this is the case, however, empathizing gives you the option of weighing all aspects of the situation fairly and making your decision based on a balanced assessment of what you've been told. Listening *without* empathy forces you to make a closed, one-sided and thus *unbalanced* decision. In addition, empathizing might help you go a little deeper and discover why continual excuses seem to be the norm for this person.

The Benefits In a Frank, Dick and Jane World

Managers who learn to listen with empathy consistently make more effective decisions and they are much more able to connect with employees when they speak. This is true because they tend to get more honest input from the people who surround them and they understand it more clearly. And this delivers a three-fold crushing blow to the Us and Them Syndrome in your organization:

1: *They* Understand

First, your sensitivity is recognized by your employees, customers and clients. They view you as a fair and balanced manager – one who is open to their ideas. This leads to a willingness to trust in your decision-making, follow your lead, and offer you ideas (including honest criticism) that can turn out to be invaluable.

2: *You* Understand

Second, as a manager with human sensitivities, you begin to understand your employees, customers and clients on a much deeper level. Listening to them below the surface gives you a true picture of how they feel and what motivates them. This enables you to communicate with (and thus satisfy) them more effectively in the future.

3: *Profit!*

Finally, as a result of the two benefits just mentioned, listening with empathy produces a more profitable bottom line, since your decisions become more accurate from a strictly business standpoint.

So the next time you find yourself frazzled, annoyed and tempted to listen to the "tip of the iceberg," take a deep breath and tell yourself the few extra seconds you're about to spend "listening below the surface" are critical to the destruction of the Us and Them Syndrome and your Frank, Dick and Jane commitment. Then, open up and let the ideas flow in… along with the empowerment they'll give you.

F D & J Bullet Plate

Power Empathy

- ✓ Let down your own OPPEX barriers
- ✓ Attempt to view the problem *from the other person's point of view*
- ✓ Do unto others…
- ✓ Empathizing Doesn't Mean You Have to Agree
- ✓ The Benefits
- ✓ They Understand
- ✓ You Understand
- ✓ Profit!

Ten:

Clarify Executive Vision

We call it executive vision: The ability to form a mental image of how a company should evolve to its full potential, including the business strategies it will take to make that evolution a reality. Without clear executive vision, senior managers can waste enormous amounts of time and energy struggling to position their companies in the intensely competitive and constantly changing marketplace.

Consider the by-products of those struggles — a justified lack of credibility and respect for the management team, the poor morale that results from repeated misfires and wasted efforts, mediocre productivity, anemic financial results, and just as damaging a healthy and growing Us and Them Syndrome!

As important as clear executive vision may be, however, we have to agree it's only half of the story. The other half is *communicating* that vision with Frank, Dick and Jane clarity to the employees who will provide the sweat, muscle and front-line momentum needed to bring it off. And that begins in the executive conference room.

By clarifying a precise understanding of the company's vision and the actions required to achieve it, the senior staff creates a kind of business target for employees. If the target is placed in the open, clearly defined and well marked, *and* if employees are given the skills and opportunities to hit the bulls-eye, chances are excellent the vision will be realized.

As we've discussed in this book, however, we may fall short in the "definition and clarification" departments. What's worse, we may not realize it. Instead, we may view the *by-products* as the root causes. Red ink in manufacturing and sales? Customer dissatisfaction? Us and Them Syndrome eroding morale? It's all due to material shortages, unexpected scheduling "challenges", untrained employees, management screw ups, union problems, turnover – all conditions which can be traced back to a poorly defined and clarified company vision.

The solution? Define and communicate an executive vision so clear, honest and precise that employees can't help but hit the bulls-eye. How? Start by putting the Frank, Dick and Jane power trio to work in your executive meetings. Here's how…

Start By Taking It Personally

As complex as today's marketplace may be, in some respects it is brutally simple. Managers and executives are only as valuable as the results they produce. To the extent you implement the Frank, Dick and Jane communication philosophy, the Us and Them Syndrome is destroyed and your results are very likely streamlined and efficient. You are able to delegate, mentor, instruct and persuade others to embrace your points of view. You are perceived as organized and "in command" by direct reports and employees at all levels of the company. In short, you exude that all important quality of leadership charisma.

To the extent you garble, omit and miscommunicate information, however, you suffer the opposite results. The Us and Them Syndrome flourishes. You and your staff may be seen as disorganized and out of touch, with questionable opinions and tentative leadership presence.

Establish a Top-Down Frank, Dick and Jane Culture

Without a culture of openness, mutual respect and fair play, employees will not trust top management. The Frank, Dick and Jane philosophy helps develop an executive staff that's trusted, approachable and most of all respected by managers and craft employees alike. And that, of course, comes from the frankness and simple clarity we've been talking about in this book. Frank, Dick and Jane managers and executives tell it like it is. They're fair and tough, but also confident, open and respected.

As a leader of these executives, your challenge, then, is to make it a part of the company's culture so all your managers and executives consider it a given. How?

Include the Frank, Dick and Jane Philosophy In Management Objectives

Professional communicators and marketers often quote one essential element in influencing people's attitudes and perceptions – *repetition*. You can guarantee that repetition and the positive results it will produce by making clear, open communication a continually reviewed mandate at all levels of your management team. Launch this mandate with a commitment by the executive staff to consider the Frank, Dick and Jane philosophy an essential part of all company business.

Now we all know that management objectives should be measurable and time sensitive. And measuring a person's commitment to Frank, Dick and Jane may be a little difficult. But there's absolutely nothing wrong with insisting that managers become knowledgeable and skilled in the Frank, Dick and Jane communication style, and it certainly can't hurt to make their communication experiences a part of the discussion at each review session.

Sharpen Focus In the Board Room

Remember our analogy about the photograph taken with an out of focus camera? The image recorded on the negative is "fuzzy" and thus useless. So it goes with executive vision and boardroom decisions. And it's worth noting that this point is absolutely critical:

If actions agreed to in executive meetings are not made simple, precise and perfectly clear at the source — among those few critical leaders who will implement and supervise all efforts aimed at hitting that business target — clearly communicating them to employees will be impossible.

As much as you might like to, you can't do it alone. And that means using the Frank, Dick and Jane skills we've covered in every executive meeting you chair or are a part of.

Present It Face To Face With "Dick and Jane" Simplicity

Once you've made the vision clear at executive levels, and the steps required to make it a reality, deliver that message to employees in person, and, above all, keep it Frank, Dick and Jane. As we've seen, nothing scrambles company communication and breeds management disrespect faster than "sophisticated" corporate-speak — business jargon the average employee can only guess at.

Resist Clichés and Facades

If you create an internal vision campaign, make it *credible*. Telling employees they are part of a "company family" may have been acceptable twenty-five years ago in the "you'll have that job for life" era, but these days all employees know perfectly well that whatever any of us chooses to call it, it's "strictly business". The same goes for the "it's not about the money" pitch. To a large degree it *is* about the money and we all know it, so why play silly games. It's in these types of communication situations that "Frank" becomes the dominant force.

For instance, instead of the "family 'business", why not ask employees to consider the achievement of the company vision a personal business investment – the business they're investing their lives in. And the pay-off for that investment? The financial success they can achieve (and hopefully share in) along with the personal satisfaction of knowing they pulled it off. Remember: In addition to a healthy paycheck, true achievers work for their own personal satisfaction, not "the good of the company". And that's fine as long as their talent and energy is focused on the company's vision.

The Usual? Well, Almost

In the end, communicating a clear executive vision is a must for any company striving to excel, and a sure-fire way to head off the Us and Them Syndrome. And pulling it off is not that much different than most other business efforts. It requires planning, plain old hard work, and a healthy dose of good old-fashioned, Frank, Dick and Jane communication.

F D & J Bullet Plate

Clarifying Executive Vision

✓ Start by taking it personally
✓ Establish a top-down culture of approachability
✓ Include communication in management objectives
✓ Sharpen focus in the Board Room
✓ Present it face-to-face with "Dick and Jane" simplicity
✓ Resist clichés and facades
✓ Role up your sleeves and dig in!

Part Three

A Few Tips from the Power Trio

With the Frank, Dick and Jane communication style under your belt, you should feel empowered to redefine your company and put the kibosh on the Us and Them Syndrome for once and for all. But is that really it? Is your communication 101 class complete? I've worked in the communication field for over thirty-five years, and I continue to learn more about this fascinating topic every day.

With that in mind, on the following pages you will find a few Frank, Dick and Jane tips that will add to your knowledge base and help you keep the Us and Them Syndrome out of your life for good!

Eleven:

Diffuse Combustible Communicators

As we've seen, your ability to listen and empathize is a critical factor in developing a solid Frank, Dick and Jane communication style. But how about the other person's ability or willingness to listen to you?

We all interact with a variety of business-related personalities — angry customers, overly demanding clients, dictatorial bosses and difficult subordinates, to name a few. And our success often depends on how well we're able to adjust to and deal with these personalities. The same is true on a personal level. People come in various communication types, and dealing with them can be extremely delicate — in fact, it can sometimes be like strapping on a flak-jacket and defusing a bomb.

Put another way, poor communications chemistry can lead to highly combustible interactions. And that in turn can detonate an otherwise profitable or productive interaction right before your eyes!

Over the years I've categorized these various "combustible" communication types, along with a few simple techniques you can use to make sure your chemistry doesn't lead to a costly verbal flare-up. They've become an integral part of the Frank, Dick and Jane philosophy, in this case with primary emphasis on our man Frank. The reason is simple. In the end, if you can't get through, it makes no difference how clear your words are. And sometimes that takes a little blunt honesty.

Following is a brief overview of each.

Idea Garblers

No, they're not speaking from underwater, but they might as well be, because these folks garble parts of what they say and mix up words and thoughts. Why? At least partly because they have the mistaken idea that you already know most of what's rolling around in their head! Idea Garblers are often busy and contemplative individuals. They may also be very intelligent, but easily "scattered" or disoriented.

Defense

When you're interacting with Idea Garblers, don't assume you can read between the lines — especially if it's an important issue. Instead, slow them down or stop them in their tracks. Be tactful but clear, and say something like, "Maybe you'd better Dick and Jane me on this. I'm not 100% clear" or, "Wait, let's go back to the beginning. I missed something." Or you might try, "Something got by me there. Can we cover that again?"

Once you feel you've got it right, feed your understanding back to them. Say something like, "Okay, now am I right in assuming that…."

Speed Rappers

We all know these people. They're the all too familiar "just the facts" types. Their concept of communication is a rapid-fire barrage that you're expected to decode in split second intervals. Speed Rappers are often too harried or scattered to slow down and communicate clearly with you. They may even realize this, but feel the communication is not that important! They can be blunt, terse, and often irritating — especially when you act on their instructions, get it wrong and end up taking the "rap".

Speed Rappers sometimes use the guise of being in a hurry as a deflector so they won't have to deal with difficult issues. If you watch and listen to them closely, you'll recognize this. It's a sure sign if they tend to suddenly speed up and get vague every time important issues are at stake.

Defense

When you're "taking fire" from a Speed Rapper, try saying, "Okay. No problem. But listen, I need just a few more facts to be clear" or, "I'll hop right on it, but I want to be sure I get this right for you. Tell me this…" and then slowly repeat what's been said. Or say, "Wait a minute. I just 'disconnected' there. Could you say that once more a little slower? I don't want to miss any of this."

PointAvoiders

As you've probably guessed, PointAvoiders just can't seem to get to the point. They deliver lots of quips, anecdotes, side-bars and other peripheral mumbo-jumbo, but very little meaningful data. They seem perfectly comfortable skirting all around the real issue, but never quite focusing on it. Meanwhile, you're going bonkers. Sometimes this is political maneuvering and sometimes an oversight. More often than not, it's just plain old poor communication skills.

Defense

Be tactful, but take PointAvoiders to the point and hold them there. You can do this by stating your understanding of the issue and requesting that they confirm it. This means guiding the discussion, but doing it in a way that doesn't offend them or appear to be overly aggressive. For instance you might say, "So here's the way I see the real issue. You want me to…." or, "You feel that I should do this. Is that right?" or, "So when we get right down to it, the real issue is…."

Meemees

Meemees have an unspoken credo – "Me, me and only me!" Though they're usually very friendly individuals, they're always jumping in and they don't really listen to much of what you have to say. The fact is, they're too obsessed with getting their own two cents in. In a Meemee's mind, his or her opinion is all that matters. Your words are just brief interruptions between their thoughts. Watch them closely and you'll notice they're always ready to jump in and pounce excitedly on your pauses so they can give you their "expert" advice.

Defense

Again, try being firm but tactful. In fact, in the case of Meemees, you may have to bring a little more of our man Frank into play. Try saying something like, "Do me a favor. I want you to listen to what I'm going to say, and don't think about your answer right away. First, just focus and listen. Okay?" Or try, "Think about this – now *really*..."or, "Okay, put your opinion aside for just a second. Can you do that?" After you've said this, look directly into their eyes for a solid mental connection. Then get your idea out fast before they slip back into their Meemee mode.

Space Heads

We all know the Space Heads. They're friendly, mellow and nice enough, but they always seem to be on some other planet. In a sense they *are* light years "away", because they're thinking about one thing as they say (or hear) another. The ever familiar vacant stare is one sure sign you're talking to a Space Head. Another reliable indicator is when you get hesitant responses like, "Ah, what?" or "Yeah, uh…right" or, "Sure….What was that, now?"

Defense

Just as with Meemees, being firm, specific and sometimes even forceful is the key. Ask your Space Head something like, "Are you distracted? Should I come back later? Because when I go over this I need your full attention." If it happens to be someone you know well, a Space Head "buddy" so to speak, you can wake them up with friendly, "Earth to Bill…" or, "Hellooo…" To be more direct you might try, "It's going to be a waste of my time to go through this unless I've got you focused on me. And I haven't got the time to waste. Okay?"

Barrier Brains

Whenever you can, try not to get into serious discussions with Barrier Brains. For them, communication is one way only – *their way*. No matter what you say, they have a defense ready to spring on you. They never stop to listen to your side or consider your point of view objectively because they're convinced their opinion is right, and it's their duty to set you straight. Though they're a lot like

Meemees, Barrier Brains are often not so nice about it. In fact, sometimes they're downright combative. They may refuse to listen even if they *don't* have an "expert" opinion. They feel it's the principle of the thing, but the fact is they're just plain old stubborn. As most of us have expereinced, many teenagers go through a protracted Barrier Brain phase.

Defense

Barrier brains often need to be given a wake-up call and unfortunately you may be the one to do it – if you want any chance of getting though, that is. Try saying, "Look, I need to be frank. I feel like you're just completely closed off. I want to *talk* about this. I want to *share* my ideas and I want to share yours. But first I have to feel like you're *really* considering what I have to say."

If that doesn't work, you might become even more blunt and try, "Is it reasonable for me to assume that as your supervisor (or parent, assistant, client, etc.) I should expect you to at least *listen* to my side of this and think about it objectively? That's what I'm after. An open conversation. Not a one-way battle or a verbal war. And that's what we have right now. We're both wasting our time. I'll make you this promise. I'll listen to your opinion fairly and openly if you'll do the same for me. Let's do this together, okay?"

But Be Sure...

Now, there is one caveat to this combustible communication "fire-fighting". Before you use any of these techniques, do a frank self-assessment. Be absolutely sure *you're* not part of the communication problem. Stop and ask yourself: Am *I* really listening? Am *I* being open and objective when it comes to *their* ideas? Am *I* communicating in a constructive and mutually productive way? If you can truthfully answer "yes" to these questions, dig in and start defusing.

No, you won't always win the battle of the Barrier Brains, Meemees, Space Heads and other combustible communicators. But if you try these techniques, you'll certainly defuse a heck of a lot more bombs than you'll set off.

Twelve:

Put a Little MIM in Your Project Meetings

Another practical example of Frank Dick & Jane communication can be illustrated in a project management technique I call MIM. That's short for **Minimum Input Management.** The MIM concept is simple...

> *Communicate crystal clear, Frank, Dick and Jane information to your project team with minimal time and effort, then reap the benefits.*

No, MIM can't make project management a cake walk. As we all know, no one with significant accountability in charge of people and company resources enjoys that luxury. But it will give you

Ray DiZazzo

and your managers the ability to clearly define and explain projects to your staffs in one relatively short, highly focused meeting.

The MIM concept is a variation of the "Tell 'em" method, with more of a corporate versus academic emphasis. Here's a look at the basic MIM steps.

Research and Organize

As we've said, one standard rule of Frank, Dick and Jane communication is to first gain focus in your own mind about what you plan to say. When it comes to MIM, you can accomplish this by thoroughly researching your project information and organizing the points you plan to make in a simple and coherent form. A brief outline can often help in the organization process. Major items are listed as topic headings and facts relating to each heading are listed below as bullets or subheadings. This will give you a clear and simple road map for your presentation. That, in turn, will manifest itself in confidence as you speak.

Chair an *Undisturbed* Kick-Off Meeting

We all put up with the usual meeting interruptions – phones, faxes, secretaries, bosses – you name it. But project launch meetings are not "the usual". A lot

122

may be riding on the short, extremely valuable period of time you will spend communicating the project to your people. For that reason, get them together in a quiet, isolated room. No phones (cell phones included). No interruptions. No other topics. If that means leaving the building or your office area – do it. Without a quiet, thoughtful atmosphere you can't expect your staff to focus clearly on your words. And before you start the meeting, let everyone know you'd like them to put all other issues aside and focus their attention strictly on the project you're about to discuss.

Start with a "Tell 'Em You're Gonna Tell 'Em" Overview

Creating a foundation should always be your first step because it gives everyone a sense of how they will fit into the big picture, and it establishes a framework they can then use to build on with your additional facts and instructions. Without this, your presentation may seem disjointed or confusing. Think of presenting your ideas *without* an overview as something like giving individuals a handful of verbal puzzle pieces and asking them to assemble the puzzle as you speak.

So what exactly do I mean by an overview? It's the "Tell 'em you're gonna tell 'em" part of the presentation — a brief statement of the key project areas or phases, along with the reasons it is being undertaken. It may also include a timeline and budget figures. An abbreviated overview of a public affairs project might be stated something like this:

> *Our mission is to develop a way to make customers aware of how we benefit the community, and to let them know about our philosophy of giving back to the people who support us. We'll do that with a four phase media plan. First, we'll design a general action plan and a timeline. Second, we'll come up with a profile of each of the charities we support and the community programs we're involved in. Third, we'll analyze what types of media would best communicate this to the people in the community, and fourth, we'll formalize our plan, produce the media and get the word out. The project starts today and our challenge is to have it up and running in six weeks.*

Follow a Logical "Tell 'em" Sequence of Progression

With your overview out of the way, as you begin describing the project in detail, arrange your ideas in a logical "Tell 'em" style order. Say something like:

> *Now that you've all got a clear picture of what we'd like to accomplish, let's take it one step at a time.*

At that point, describe the individual steps, phases and employee assignments as they will logically occur. And don't be afraid to go into considerable detail. Better to say a little too much than have your employees unsure of their specific responsibilities.

Delay Verbal Sidebars for Out of Sequence Information

One of the challenges you'll face with many project launches is clarifying non-linear information – facts and figures that don't fit neatly together into that logical sequence just mentioned.

As an example, suppose phase one of the project links to phase four in some critical way. It's important to let your employees know that, of course, but don't

125

break your logical sequence to explain it. Instead, make it a delayed sidebar. When you come to that issue, simply say:

> *Now this has an important effect on phase four, but I want to come back to that after we've gotten the bigger picture so we can see how it fits in.*

A statement like this puts employees on alert for your sidebar at a later time, but it doesn't cloud the issue at the moment. Later, when you get to that point, you can refer back to your comment. Or, if you feel this would break the logical flow of your presentation, you may decide to move through the entire project presentation and make a second pass through it to discuss the indirect issues that are critical.

Trim Out the Jargon

Corporate jargon can be very confusing and irritating. Consider the following statement:

> *Our charter is to implement a multi-level sales program which we anticipate will increase lagging sales revenues*

substantially and bolster our product image perception in the eyes of our customers.

A few minutes of this kind of talk – in logical order or not – will glaze over your employees faster than a good hypnotist. And what will they get from the meeting? Bored! Instead, try using simple, active word choices that give employees plenty of detail and a visual sense of what you mean. In the case just mentioned, you might try something like:

We have two simple aims with this project: First, to bring sales revenues up by twenty percent, and second, to make our products plain old irresistible to our customers.

This is Frank, Dick and Jane-speak – clear, descriptive and much more real world than the "corporate" version. One tip for trimming jargon is to give an advance copy of your meeting notes to a colleague or secretary. Ask for an objective critique and explain that clarity and simplicity are your primary goals. Since much of your meeting will be presented verbally, you might also try a rehearsal, paying close attention to how clearly you're stating your facts.

Look for "Light Bulbs," Summarize, and Ask for Feedback

During your presentation watch your employees' eyes, body language and gestures. Do they seem alert and nod periodically, signaling they understand? Do they ask occasional questions, indicating they're involved? Do *you* have a comfortable sense that the light bulbs are clicking on? Or do you find yourself facing quizzical or dazed looks, or employees looking down or away from you? If you're getting the latter, stop occasionally to summarize (a good idea in any case) and then say, "Clear?" or "Any questions?" or "Okay, how about some feedback. I want to be absolutely sure we're all on the same wavelength."

Q & A to Close

Answering questions during your meeting is fine, provided they are minimal, focused on the topic at hand and you can deal with them quickly. In-depth questions should be tabled for scheduled intervals or immediately following your talk.

In any case, don't allow the meeting to adjourn without a frank, open, Q & A session. And once this is completed, be absolutely sure everyone is clear and focused before they leave. If you feel a certain individual may be confused but hesitant to speak up, have that person stay for a short time to discuss their role in private. If any questions are left unresolved, be sure a specific time frame is established to resolve them – and, of course, follow through.

Got it? Planning on using the structure of simplicity? If there's any question left in your mind, remember this:

> *A lack of this type of simple structure causes thousands of misunderstandings in even the most sophisticated business meetings, and these misunderstandings result in billions of dollars lost annually due to confusion, rework, poor productivity, resentment and frustration. And they also nurture the mistrust and contempt that are the seeds of the Us and Them Syndrome*

That's right. As educated and sophisticated as we may be, we often ignore the simple basics of clear communication and replace it with fragmented or rambling presentations overloaded with jargon, tangents, content "dead-ends" and confusing idea patterns.

The result?

Us and Them.

Thirteen:

A Matter of "Record"

Remember the old stackable 78 RPM turntables? A metal rod jutted straight up, out of the center, and groups of LP (long playing) albums could be stacked on top. As each album finished, a small trigger on the rod would release an album down onto the turntable and the needle would swing back into the groove. Non-stop music for hours!

Now imagine we each have a stackable turntable up top – that's right, in our consciousness. But instead of albums, we stack up ideas – issues we have to deal with. The dog. The house. The report. Lunch (Oh, man, lunch!) The productivity numbers. The person who just walked up to your desk and is now waiting to be heard.

In our case, however, not only are we stacking up ideas, our stacks have a unique quality. They can instantaneously be rearranged.

Think about it. You're focused on budget numbers and your boss drops a note on your desk. What do you do? The numbers "LP album" pops back into the stack, and the note "album" drops onto the turntable. As you're reading the note, the phone rings. You pick it up and the employee you disciplined this morning is on the phone. She says she quits and she's walking out the door at that moment. The boss's note "LP album" goes back into the stack, and the "Oh wow. What do I do now?" album drops onto the turntable....

The point? Everyone has a constant flow of ideas floating around up top and they're switching focus continually, especially when things are busy at work. It stands to reason, then, that if you're trying to speak to someone and you allow this continual reshuffling to take place, regardless of how clearly you've focused your message it, will not hit home. The listener may get parts of it or a kind of murky, tip of the iceberg understanding of it in between waves of shifting ideas, but the true clarity of the message will be lost.

Now ask yourself how many times this happens. How often is it going on in the important interactions you're involved in? Not that often, you say? Remember, people often *appear* to be tuned in, but they may have "LPs" dropping in, one after another as you speak.

So how do you avoid this very common communication trap? Here are three simple tools:

1. **Interest**
2. **Importance**
3. **A request for the listener's undivided attention**

Sound simple? It is. Amazingly simple. The problem is, most us are too busy to think about using these very effective little "attention getters". We just keep rapping right along, spitting out idea after idea, never questioning whether they're getting through or not.

Here's how they work.

If you speak to someone who's not tuned in, your message is completely or partially lost. Period. But if you tell someone that what you have to share is *interesting*, there's a better chance you're going to get a mental connection: "Hey, Jan, I heard something really interesting yesterday."

If you tell them it's *important*, your chances are even better: "You know, David, I came across something very important to you."

But if you simply *ask for their attention* you're going to score a hit.

How is it done? Again, simple. Look the person straight in the eye, pause and say, "John, do me a favor. Put everything else aside and focus on me. This is important." With that kind of a statement prefacing your message, you're guaranteed to lock in wavelengths. To assure yourself, continue to look deep into the person's eyes as you say it. Don't look away. Mental connection is the kind of thing that's visible in the baby blues. Is it there? A tuned in psyche? An assurance your message is going to sail straight across the abyss and sink in just as you wanted it to?

If so, fire away.

If not, don't spill the beans 'till you get it. Say, "I can see that you can't focus right now. I've got something that you need to hear and focus on clearly. When you're ready to give me your undivided attention, let me know."

If that doesn't do it, chances are very good this person is a lost cause at the moment, and you simply won't get through to him or her.

Think about it.

If you focused your message you set up a crystal clear thought stream that you intended to send to another individual. And if you've now gotten that person on the same wavelength, he or she is perfectly tuned in and ready to accept and interpret you message – clearly.

Fourteen:

Image-Speak

Speaking of messages, do poetry and business communication have anything in common? Unless you happen to be a famous songwriter or author, you'd probably say, "No way." As business communicators, however, there is at least one bit of "literary wisdom" we can all learn from the poets. It's a simple technique that will help get your ideas across with a lot more punch and pizzazz – especially when giving presentations or speaking to large groups. I call it Image-Speak.

What-Speak?

Image-Speak. It means speaking in a way that creates mental images in the mind of a listener or reader. Image-Speak can be a valuable communication tool in everyday conversations and written material, but it's especially effective when you're speaking in front of a group.

As an example, consider the short blurb below. Imagine a person speaking about himself in front of an audience...

> *I feel I have great communication skills. I've worked very hard on them over the years, and today I view myself as a communication professional.*

Does this get the point across? Sure it does. It's clear and simple. But it has no imagery – no oomph! As a result, the words just kind of drift out to the audience and pass "in one ear and out the other" – in a very unmemorable way.

But suppose the speaker said it this way:

> *I think of my communications skills as something like a powerful magnifying glass. And I take pride in focusing crystal clear ideas in the minds of my listeners.*

What's different about this version? It's more colorful and memorable because it uses the analogy of a "... magnifying glass..." to visualize the point. It's Image-Speak. Granted, you may not want to run around your company offices spouting "poetic"

Image-Speak at every turn. But on those occasions when you want your words to be vivid and engaging, it can be very effective. As I said, that's especially true when you're delivering motivational speeches.

So How Is It Done?

Image-Speak requires finding memorable analogies and making visual connections that give your ideas fresh, vivid qualities. A few good examples are those we discussed in the "Penetrate OPPEX" chapter:

Straight Version	**Image-Speak Analogy**
Our customer service plan is quite lethargic.	This customer service plan is inching along like a snail in a coma.
Our employee motivation program is gaining momentum every day.	Our employee motivation program is rolling through this company like a tidal wave of positive energy.
This was the most productive sales campaign we've ever undertaken.	This started as a sales campaign, and turned into a truckload of profit headed straight for the bank!

Care for a A Few More Examples?

Straight Version	**Image-Speak Analogy**
Our sales figures have been declining for months	Our sales figures are in a five month nose dive!
We need to get some new thinking going in this company	We need to open the creative flood gates and let the new ideas flow in.
We need to be a competitive force in order to succeed	To win, we need to be lean, mean and hungry as hell!

Game to Try It?

Why not give it a shot. Then the next time you're scheduled to speak, your words won't lull your audience into a trance. Instead they'll, "…punch out your ideas like a heavyweight", or maybe, "…drive your message home like a dragster in high gear!" Or even….

Well, like I said, you get the point.

Fifteen:

Words Under Glass

Everything we've covered in this book has revolved around communicating messages with clarity. And the mode of communication has been exclusively verbal. Now think in terms of writing.

And let's use the magnifying glass image again. Imagine your written words becoming images under a magnifying glass. Think of your readers as viewers who hold up that glass and peer through at the idea images you create.

When you convey your ideas skillfully, they're perfectly clear under the glass and very vivid to your readers. When your writing skills aren't so refined, the images are certainly still visible to your readers, but they're not nearly as focused or easily understood.

I normally come across two styles of writing that make for great examples of what you might call this "magnifying glass" premise:

Complex Passive
Simple Active

Both styles create different types of images "under the glass" and are thus more or less effective at communicating ideas.

To illustrate, let's take the case of a new hotshot manager named John Mitchell. John was hired a month ago, he's been doing a super job, and his boss wants to convey that idea in one part of memo he's writing to his staff. Let's look at how that part of the memo might appear "under the glass" in each of the two styles we just mentioned.

Complex Passive

The newest senior member of our staff, Senior Project Manager John Mitchell, is adept at managing his workload; e.g. the many projects critical to our departmental success. Also, due to a highly professional appearance, John displays an image in keeping with our conservative corporate culture. John's employees perceive him as a manager with a keen sense of recognition and true appreciation for a job well done. Thus, in a period of one short month, John has earned a highly respected and critical position on our management team.

Obviously, this first version is "formal", "corporate" and "official" sounding. But is it simple? Active? Direct? Does the image it conveys of John appear focused and vivid under the glass? Or is it a "cloudy", "murky" image, partially obscured amongst all the cumbersome words and passive phrases like, "....adept at managing his workload; e.g. the many projects critical to our departmental success" and "...due to his highly professional appearance..." and "...he is a manager with a keen sense of recognition and true appreciation for a job well done."

Now let's assume the same boss sits down to communicate these ideas idea, but his writing skills are more polished....

Simple Active

John Mitchell, our new Senior Project Manager, dresses sharp, manages projects like a master juggler, and treats his people with a respect they'll thrive on. In one short month, John has become, not just an important member of our team, but an essential one.

This second version is simple, active and direct. It uses common but descriptive word choices and visual analogies like "...dresses sharp, manages projects like a master juggler..." to help describe John. These aren't terribly original ideas, but they are much more visual than the complex passive version. As a result, when a reader's eyes take in these words the image under the glass is a clean and sharp one — a more vivid and compelling portrayal of this new manager.

Try the Focus Factor

Try using this "under the glass" mind-set to clearly focus your ideas. Imagine your readers will "see" what you say more or less clearly based strictly on the style you choose. For Simple Active, choose verbs and nouns over adjectives. Make your sentences brief and direct. And take the time to consider more descriptive words if your first choices seem uncomfortable. A good thesaurus can be indispensable when doing this.

Stay away from the Complex Passive by limiting "to be" and "there are" type verb phrases. "It is to be determined" gives us nothing to imagine or visualize. "John will decide", on the other hand, attaches the decision to someone we know. "There are new programs to be implemented", again, gives us a passive, clouded image. "We're launching some great new programs" activates the ideas and attaches them to things we can visualize.

Remember

When you convey ideas with vague or complex word choices they may still be visible under the glass, but think of them as clouded or fuzzy around the edges. Your readers will probably still "get" your ideas, but not without some extra mental gymnastics.

If they're simple, direct and active, however, your listeners or readers will find a vivid, focused version of your ideas under the glass and thus crystal clear communication.

Finally! Us and Us!

Managing any business is difficult at best.

A dynamic stream of influences are continually placing pressures on managers at all levels. Employees perceive many of these pressures, but from a different perspective. And, as we've discovered, it is the difference in these perspectives that nurtures the Us and Them Syndrome.

While learning the basics of clear and honest communication cannot be considered a panacea (panaceas simply do not exist in business), it can be recognized as one of the most powerful tools a management team possesses in achieving the company's goals and realizing the executive vision.

Aside from the formal business of achieving goals and objectives and, of course, nurturing a healthy bottom line, we must also come back to the less tangible but equally important issue of the Us and Them Syndrome – the destructive attitude that makes business progress so difficult and cumbersome.

With Frank, Dick and Jane in place in your business, the syndrome will be effectively diffused.

There will be no room for rumors because employees will be well informed and trusting of the information they've been given. The grapevine will be uprooted and minimized for the exact same reasons. Information will be readily available, clear, concise and up front.

Perhaps most important of all will be the simple fact that employees will possess a comfortable and energized feeling of belonging. They will understand their fit in the organization and, as a result, experience the enormous pride of contribution and ownership. From that will come loyalty and dedication, determination, and the self-satisfaction of knowing they truly are making a difference.

And at that point, Frank Dick and Jane would probably sum it all up in a few simple words…

"See the competition run!"

Appendix:

The Frank Dick & Jane Bullet Plate Summary

A content outline summary that will help you easily reference the Frank, Dick and Jane communication style.

Recalibrate Your Perception

- ✓ Acknowledge the profound importance and power of clear communications
- ✓ Objectively think through how you and your people communicate
- ✓ Commit to Frank, Dick and Jane as a company or departmental standard and a basic communication philosophy

Focus Your Message at the Source

- ✓ Clarify in your own mind what you plan to say

Ray DiZazzo

- ✓ Analysis: Think out what you want to communicate and what outcome you want
- ✓ Objectivity: Communicate without the distortion of emotion

Penetrate OPPEX

- ✓ Communication is distorted by individual preferences, opinions and past experiences, or OPPEX
- ✓ To limit his distortion, use precise visual language
- ✓ Eliminate corporate mumbo-jumbo
- ✓ Use analogies
- ✓ Fill in the blanks
- ✓ Ask for feedback
- ✓ Restate when necessary

Practice the Structure of Simplicity

- ✓ Carefully structure what you say using a logical flow
- ✓ Use the "Tell' em" technique

Try the Why Technique

- ✓ Always explain *why* – whether the news is good or bad
- ✓ Don't use why as an excuse, but do use it to clarify

- ✓ Don't be afraid to ask for the why – on the job and in your personal life

Power Empathy
- ✓ Let down your own OPPEX barriers
- ✓ Attempt to view the problem *from the other person's point of view*
- ✓ Do unto others…
- ✓ Empathizing doesn't mean you have to agree
- ✓ The Benefits:
    - ◦ They understand
    - ◦ You understand
    - ◦ Profit!

Clarify Executive Vision
- ✓ Start by taking it personally
- ✓ Establish a top-down culture of approachability
- ✓ Include communication in management objectives
- ✓ Sharpen focus in the Board Room
- ✓ Present it face-to-face with "Dick and Jane" simplicity
- ✓ Resist clichés and facades
- ✓ Role up your sleeves and dig in!

Acknowledgements

I'd like to thank my good friend Andy Boyer for lending his sharp editorial eye and seasoned business sense on this project. Thanks, also, goes to Neal Spruce, a fantastic boss, a savvy business leader and a darn good guy. The support of my family, especially my wife, Patti, is a critical, underlying element in every project I take on. The wonderful, iconic Dick and Jane characters, which were the inspiration for two thirds of my "Power Trio", are published under the trademark of Addison-Wesley Educational Publishers, Inc., and "*A Storybook Treasury of Dick and Jane and Friends*" is available from Grosset & Dunlap. Finally, I'd like to thank Judy Perkins, Kathy Greaves, Jesus Lopez-Varela, and the staff at Oxnard Adult School for allowing and encouraging me to share some of my ideas on communication with their amazing students.

www.ingramcontent.com/pod-product-compliance
Lightning Source LLC
Chambersburg PA
CBHW032303210326
41520CB00047B/1056